I0052823

A Coach Approach
to Leadership

A Coach Approach to Leadership

Enhancing Performance, Empowering Others

J. Val Hastings, MCC
Trigena H. Halley, PCC

Val – 1.877.381.2672, val@coaching4todaysleaders.com

Trigena – 1.801.915.4046, trigena@me.com

Website: www.coaching4todaysleaders.com

Copyright © 2010 Coaching4Today's Leaders, J. Val Hastings, and Trigena H. Halley. All rights reserved. No part of this publication shall be reproduced or transmitted in any form or by any electronic, mechanical, photocopying or recording means, or otherwise, including information storage and retrieval systems without permission in writing from the copyright holder.

ISBN # 978-0-9886128-9-1

Published in the USA

Table of Contents

Acknowledgments vii

Introduction ix

Chapter One: Getting Started as a Coach 1

Chapter Two: The Eight Building Blocks of Coaching 11

Chapter Three: A Five-Step Coaching Model 37

Chapter Four: Coaching Scenarios 41

Chapter Five: Your Next Step 45

Chapter Six: Additional Coaching Techniques and Strategies 47

Appendix A: Top Questions 51

Appendix B: Recommended Reading 57

References 59

About the Authors..61

Acknowledgments

This book is dedicated to those who have empowered me as a person, a pastor, a leader and a professional coach.

To my wife, Wendy, who continually encourages me to pursue my dreams! Thank you for your support and encouragement. What a gift you have given me. I love you.

To my parents, Val, Senior, and Audrey Hastings, who were my first real coaches. Thank you for empowering me in the ways that you parented me. Thank you for bringing out the best in me and for seeing more in me than I saw in myself at times.

To my father, Val, Senior, who modeled and mentored me in leadership. Thank you for the many, many hours we spoke of leadership and how to best empower others. I benefited much from our time together.

To my two daughters, Bryanna and Shelby, my sources of pride and joy. I love being your father.

To my editor, Linda Dessau, thank you for bringing my ideas to light and helping me clarify and polish my message.

To my Online Business Manager and Virtual Assistant, Laura Pumo, and her team at Office DEVA, thank you for pulling this together for me. Your assistance was invaluable.

To MileStone Bank, who continues to support the work of Coaching4Clergy and Coaching4Businessleaders. To all of the individuals, teams and business leaders that I have coached, this book is filled with what you have taught me. Others will benefit from you.

A special Thank You to Trigena H. Halley who reviewed this book and provided me with valuable feedback and suggestions.

Introduction

In 1999 I met my first coach. I'm embarrassed to say this, but my initial response to her was, "What sport do you coach?" After her light laughter, she explained to me she coached individuals and organizations. I was intrigued. That intrigue has grown over the years into a global vision. The vision is that every leader has coach training in their professional toolkit. Your participation in this coach training event is helping this vision become a reality.

You may be wondering the motivation behind my vision. Like many of you, I am aware of the growing number of leaders who are overwhelmed and feel ineffective and unproductive. Add to this the alarming number of today's organizations that are faltering or near closing.

Actually, there's a reason behind all of this. We are in the midst of a paradigm shift that involves moving others forward powerfully by coaching rather than directing. Leader's today must be prepared to coach individuals and teams forward in a way that creates awareness, supports solution development and invokes action and accountability on the part of the individual and the team. It is about empowering, not directing, individuals and teams to move forward effectively. Jack Welch once said "People who are coaches will be the norm. Other people won't get promoted." Coaching is a powerful tool for every leader. It is a tool that will set you apart as a leader and will provide your team a competitive advantage.

A coaching approach is one way to embrace this paradigm shift and can have a tremendous impact, not only on those you lead and support as a coach, but also on the larger organization. The coaching skills contained in this book will help you gain greater clarity about how to use coaching as a part of your leadership skill set.

At its core, coaching is about empowering others. What if empowering and equipping people became the norm in your team or with the leaders of your organization? Consider the impact this would have individually and organizationally.

Whatever (or whoever) motivated you to learn more about coaching, I want to thank you for taking this step. You are beginning a journey that will add tremendously to your life, the lives of others, your career and your organization.

Congratulations on taking this first step. Let's begin.

Chapter One
What Is Coaching?

When people discover I am coach, they usually ask me what coaching is. As I start to explain, I usually observe a combination of confusion and intrigue in my listener. Coaching, while powerful and transformational, is hard for many to understand. One person has told me on several occasions that she believes the real reason people hire me as their coach is because they like the way my voice sounds on the phone. Others have hired me as their coach saying, "I don't know what coaching is, but whatever you did for ____ (another individual), I want you to do that for me."

I still chuckle at one leader's response to my explanation of coaching: "So let me get this straight. You're going to do lots of listening, you're not going to tell me what to do nor are you going to try to fix me. I'm going to do all the work AND I'm going to pay you. I don't think so!"

Over the years I've discovered the best way to help someone understand coaching is to give them a firsthand experience of coaching. That's why I give a LIVE demonstration at the beginning of every coach training event I facilitate. Then I invite the participants to define what coaching is, based on what they have just witnessed.

Let's define what coaching is and what it is not. The International Coach Federation (www.coachfederation.org) defines coaching as "partnering with clients in a thought-provoking and creative process that inspires them to maximize their personal and professional potential." (International Coach Federation).

Here is how I define coaching: As a coach, I help people get the results they want by bringing out the best in them. I'll also explain that coaching isn't about fixing people or solving problems, rather coaching is a developmental or discovery-based process. Similar to athletic coaches, we further develop the skill and talent already inherent in the people we coach.

Whether you use the International Coach Federation definition of coaching, my definition or develop your own there are several key components I want to highlight:

1. Coaching is a partnership.

The coach and the coachee are involved in a collaborative process that is 100% about the person being coached. The relationship between the coach and coachee is of utmost importance. Safety and trust in this relationship create an environment in which fresh perspectives and new ways of being can be explored. A coachee is more likely to let you see who they really are if they believe they can trust you.

This is so important for today's leaders, many of whom report they are overwhelmed, exhausted, and generally overworked. In fact, on more than one occasion, I've had leaders and individuals report that there is no one they trust, nor anyone they feel close to. If nothing else, the rise of coaching will provide today's leaders with a safe person to talk with. And that's a big win!

2. Coaching accelerates what is already underway or about to begin.

This is a key distinction between coaching and other disciplines. Because our perspective is that the person is already whole and complete, we're not moving immediately into fix-it mode or bringing a scarcity mentality. Instead we look for clues and dig for treasures in what we see in front of us. Coaches enjoy spending time at the intersection of curiosity and wonder.

So many of the individuals and teams I coach initially have little or no awareness of what is already underway or about to begin. One of the benefits of the coaching process is that it creates space in the coachee's schedule–even if it's only 30 minutes–to step back and see what is underway or about to begin. Through deep listening and powerful questions the coach helps the other person gain greater clarity about what they really want and what goals and strategy they need to employ to get there.

"The greatest good you can do for another is not just to share your riches, but to reveal to him his own." —Benjamin Disraeli

Coaches help people see what they have to offer others and their organization.

3. Coaches maximize potential, moving people from good to great.

Coaches do more than inspire or cheer on; coaches help people develop and actually make forward progress. Have you ever heard of a masterful athlete who achieved any success without coaching? A coach will develop you further, faster and deeper than you could ever do on your own.

One of the ways we maximize potential in coaching is by tapping into the greatness of those we coach. Coaches intentionally look for and develop the strengths and giftedness of the person being coached. I appreciate the way in which Benjamin Zander explains this in his book The Art of Possibility.

Zander begins each term by informing his students they already have an A. Our coachees also begin with an A. (We'll talk a little more about Ben Zander later in this book.)

In Zander's approach, every student begins with an "A", and as such the teacher is able to focus on and recognize the learner's potential and bring it forth to fruition. The analogy that is made is of Michelangelo, who sees a masterpiece in each block of marble and believes his job is to bring that beauty to the surface. This is how Zander's sees the role of leaders, teachers, coaches and other individuals who develop talent.

As coaches we can adopt the practice of "giving an A" by looking for and leveraging the strengths and potential of those we coach. That perspective will frame our assumptions, the information we attend to, the decisions we make and how we approach those we are coaching.

In the Zander example, the only requirement for actually obtaining the "A" is each learner must write a letter that details why he/she received the "A". At the beginning of the class Zander announces, "Each student in this class will get an 'A' for this course. However there is one requirement that you must fulfill to earn this grade: Sometime during the next two weeks, you must write me a letter dated next May (end of the semester), which begins with the words, 'Dear Mr. Zander, I got my "A" because...' And in this letter you are to tell, in as much detail as you can, the story of what will have happened to you by next May that is in line with this extraordinary grade."

By doing this Zander focuses on the person they will become – this is where we as coaches should be spending most of our time – moving individuals from where they are to where they want to be – coaching the "gap."

Another way that coaches maximize potential is by looking beyond solutions to shifts. Shift work involves internal perspectives, beliefs and assumptions. I like to tell people that as a coach I "shine a flashlight" on their perspectives, beliefs and assumptions and help them see how these support and limit their forward progress. Let me give you an example. Many years ago I changed careers, from being a pastor to being a coach. I had a belief that no one would hire a pastor as their coach. There were no external solutions or action plans that could adequately address this internal belief. Instead, my coach helped me create an awareness of how this internal belief was limiting me, plus he helped me gain an entirely new perspective on this belief.

Eventually, one day the shift happened and I saw the same thing completely differently. All of a sudden I just knew that there were people who would want to hire me as their coach because I was a pastor. That was all that was needed. A giant leap forward followed.

Another way that coaches maximize the potential of others is to walk beside them, rather than trying to lead them. The other person remains in the driver's seat, but the coach is invited along for the ride. I really like this expression: A coach is not a sage on the stage, but a guide alongside. How true!

We fully help others develop their potential, but not by doing for them or telling them what to do. In this role of "guide alongside" the coach becomes:

- Your partner in achieving professional and personal goals.
- Your sounding board when making decisions.
- Your support in professional and personal development.
- Your guide in communication and life skills.
- Your motivation when strong actions are needed.
- Your unconditional supporter when you take a hit.

How is Coaching Different from Therapy, Consulting and Mentoring?

Let me first say that coaching is not the "be all and end all" of helping people. While there are tremendous benefits to coaching, the same is true of therapy, consulting and mentoring. All are of value. Taking that a step further, I believe it is absolutely essential we, as coaches, appreciate the important contributions that therapists, consultants and mentors make to the ongoing success of those we coach. In fact, about a third of those I coach are also using the services of a therapist, consultant or mentor.

During a break at a training event I was facilitating, there was a consultant in the group—obviously hot under the collar—who stated that because I was training all these people to be coaches, no one would need him anymore. My response to him was I believed just the opposite. That as the coaching industry grows, more and more individuals and organizations are recognizing there are times when the expertise of a consultant, therapist or mentor are exactly what is needed. I don't think he believed me.

Second, there is much overlap between coaching and therapy, consulting and mentoring. Consultants identify with the brainstorming, designing the plan and follow-through elements of the coaching process, while mentors relate to our "guide alongside" philosophy. During a recent coach training event for therapists, a participant stated many of the listening concepts and skills he was learning were very similar to what he learned as a therapist. Another marriage and family therapist defined coaching as "therapy for healthy people" and declared how refreshing it would be to work with people who were basically whole and complete.

Third, many coaches see the benefits of combining coaching with these other treatment modalities. A perfect example is the mentor-coaching I offer coaches. Those I mentor-coach benefit from the access I have to both mentoring and coaching skills and techniques. Sometimes I blend the two; other times I use one or the other. There are also many consultants and therapists who now blend coaching into their practices. Note that it is very important to clearly understand the similarities and the differences when intentionally overlapping coaching with another discipline or skill set.

Fourth, coaching is still new enough that there are many competing perceptions about what it is. Someone who offers coaching may or may not be adhering to the techniques and approaches you are learning here. I once attended a coach training event where the trainer stated when he works with his clients, "I just tell them what to do. That's what they are paying me for." That's definitely NOT how we define coaching around here!

Coaching versus Therapy

Over the years, I have gathered several key distinctions between coaching and therapy. One distinction is that therapy is about recovery, while coaching is about discovery. For the most part, therapy is about recovering from a pain or dysfunction, often arising from the past. The focus is on recovering overall psychological health.

Coaching, on the other hand, assumes an overall level of health and wellness and therefore isn't focused on recovery, rather discovery. The coaching process happens in an environment of curiosity and wonder as we seek peak performance in those we coach. Using a timeline, therapy is usually recovering from the past, bringing the person into a healthy present. Coaches begin in the healthy present and launch out to create and discover the future.

Another helpful distinction is archaeology versus architecture. Therapy, like archaeology, digs into the past to uncover hidden meanings that help us understand both the past and the present. Coaching, similar to architecture, builds on the solid, healthy foundation of the person as they are today, with the primary focus to design, create and support. I often remind new coaches that unless there is forward progress, or signs that forward progress is coming, it's not really coaching.

One more distinction: therapy versus therapeutic. Many individuals and groups report the therapeutic benefits of coaching; they generally feel more positive about themselves and their present and future as a result of coaching. Yes! It feels good to really make progress and actually accomplish what you set out to accomplish. Coaching is therapeutic, but it's not therapy. Those who coach have an ethical obligation to make referrals for therapy when needed. Indicators may include:

- An increase in overall sadness
- Difficulty focusing
- Changes in sleep patterns, appetite and anger
- Feelings of hopelessness
- An increase of risk-taking behavior
- Thoughts of suicide

Coaching versus Consulting

There are two questions that come to my mind when I consider the distinction between coaching and consulting:

- Who is the recognized expert?
- Who is responsible for the outcome?

In consulting, the recognized expert is the consultant. Most people work with a consultant because they believe the consultant's expertise will benefit them or their organization. Usually the consultant helps diagnose problems and prescribes a set of solutions. In coaching, the recognized expert is the person or team being coached. The coaching perspective is that the coachee is capable of generating their own solutions. The role of the coach is to provide a discovery-based framework that taps further into the expertise of the person being coached.

In fact, sometimes the biggest contribution I make to another person is three simple words: "I don't know." It is by being open to not knowing that a coach propels the coachee forward.

As far as who is responsible for the outcome, in consulting, the consultant is responsible for the desired outcome. By following the consultant's advice, their client will achieve their desired outcome. Contrast this with coaching. Coaches seek to empower the one being coached; it is the coachee who is doing the work and is responsible for the outcome; they generate their own plans and take their own actions. The coach is responsible for holding the framework of the coaching process, but not for the outcome.

Coaching versus Mentoring

Mentoring is a process of guiding another along a path that you (the mentor) have already traveled. The sharing or guidance includes experiences and learning from the mentor's own experience. The underlying premise is the insight and guidance of the mentor can accelerate the learning curve of the one being mentored. Although in many instances a coach and coachee might share a similar experience, it is not the coach's personal and professional experience that is of greatest value. In the coaching relationship it is the coachee's experiences that are of most importance.

Does that mean that the coach never shares their experiences or expertise? Not at all. At a recent International Coach Federation (ICF) conference I learned one of the things that coachees value most from their coach is when the coach shares advice and experience when asked for and when appropriate. Notice those qualifiers—when asked for and when appropriate.

When coachees come right out and ask me to tell them what to do, I usually preface any reply by saying something like, "Based on those that I have coached, in a similar situation, here are a few ideas. What do you think?" In other words, I'm holding my advice lightly—remembering that it's my best-guess opinion and nothing more.

When is it appropriate to share our experiences and expertise? Sometimes the person we are coaching may be genuinely stuck and offering advice may serve to prime the pump and get them thinking. Another time may be when a bigger goal can be met more quickly and effectively if they can leap over things of lesser importance. In all of these cases though, it is presumed that you have already established a coaching relationship of trust and safety, and you are both clear that this is only your opinion.

Initially, I recommend that new coaches refrain from offering advice. Most people have learned how to offer advice in ways that are not helpful and in fact, disempowering of others. First, we must learn how not to give advice. Then, we can begin to learn anew the art of advising. We'll talk more about this later in the book.

What Does a Typical Coaching Session Look Like?

In this hypothetical coaching scenario, a leader stated,

> "We're stuck! We've tried everything and nothing seems to work. We have the BIG picture … but can't seem to get started. The result is that we're losing momentum. It feels like we're taking one step

forward and then two steps backwards. Leaders are bailing. I'm beginning to question my ability to lead. Help!"

A coach might employ one of these five strategies:

1. **Ask the leader to say more.** One of the best places to begin is to simply invite the person to share further.

2. **Mirror back what you are hearing and observing.** It is amazing how helpful the simple act of mirroring can be. For the coachee, it is very beneficial to hear what they are saying and see how they are being.

3. **Invite the leader to describe the vision or BIG picture.** In this scenario the leader states that "We have the BIG picture...but can't seem to get started." As the coach, I want to confirm that they really do have the BIG picture. Over and over again, I discover that leaders think others have the BIG picture when they really don't. As a next step, I might encourage this leader to facilitate more conversation about the vision. The group may have been too quick to move into strategy mode, and really need to hang out a bit more with the vision.

4. **Ask about the plan.** This could very well be an implementation issue. It's not uncommon to develop a wonderful vision, hang it on the wall and assume it will just happen. A vision needs a plan. One of the top reasons a vision is never implemented is that it lacks a plan or the plan is poorly communicated.

5. **Ask about their support system.** Who can help them with this? In addition to a coach, other leaders and individuals can be of tremendous assistance. There are numerous colleagues who have valuable insights and learning from similar experiences. Tap into their experiences or seek them out for a sounding board and an encouraging word.

What Do You Mean by a "Coach Approach" to Leadership?

A growing number of today's leaders are pursing coach training as a way of enhancing the mission and vision of their organization. Many are viewing coaching as a tangible way to address their role in their organization's "talent development" process. Tom Peters, author of The Circle of Innovation, puts it this way:

"People stuff is the only stuff! Top CEOs, though they may be so-called visionaries, typically report that three-quarters or more of their time is spent on 'people stuff" (like nurturing top talent). Welcome to the club. Don't fight it! Join it! Study it! Obsess on it!"

Coach training offers practical and proven tools and skills to develop individuals and focus on the "people stuff!"

One way to incorporate coaching into your leadership style is by coaching the individuals and teams you work with, instead of taking a more traditional leadership role. We can help these teams to gain clarity about what they really, really want, then get out their way and let them make that happen. What is the result of this coaching approach to leading a team? You get a more effective team whose members are working from their strengths and greatness, rather than their weaknesses.

When we supervise and evaluate others, imagine giving them an "A" before they even start. How much more empowering and effective would that be to others? Add to that the powerful questions we ask and the deep listening we offer and we have a recipe for success.

Our organizations are filled with people experiencing personal, professional, family and physical transition and can greatly benefit from the coaching approach of support, clarity and accountability. Imagine if your teams were led by an environment of support and trust, with leaders who were skilled to bring out the best in others. Personal transformation and life change are bound to follow.

The other day a new coach said to me he believed coaching was really a luxury for leaders, especially in this economy. My response: Effective leadership is not a luxury, but a necessity. Imagine the difference in you and your organization if you partnered with a coach whose sole purpose was to bring out the very best in you and help you to continually perform at peak level. If organizations are going to fulfill their vision and have a positive global impact, then coaching must not be seen as a luxury, rather a necessity.

Chapter Two
The Building Blocks of Coaching

One of my favorite sections in any bookstore is the "How to" section. It's amazing how many "How to" books there are, and they cover an endless array of topics: how to build a deck, fix your car, knit, cook, find your perfect mate, etc.

This section is your coaching "How to." Over the next several pages, you will discover the core competencies and skills of coaching—called the "Building Blocks." These building blocks will provide a framework for your coaching.

1. Deep Listening

All coaching begins with listening!

Don't read any further until you really, REALLY get this. It all begins with listening. Far too often we take listening for granted. How many times has someone tried to help you by offering you a solution, without hearing what the problem was? They mean well, but they aren't really helpful. Years ago, I had a medical doctor who would listen to me describe my symptoms for about 13 seconds and then he would begin backing out the door, prescribing before I'd finished. I quickly learned the art of standing in the doorway.

So coaching begins with listening—deep listening. The quality of our listening has a direct bearing on the quality of our coaching. We can't draw out the best in another person, or tap into their greatness, if we haven't listened for it.

Listening is one of the greatest gifts that you can offer another person. Listening, in and of itself, provides tremendous benefits. Consider the following case study:

Nancy Kline provided an opportunity for every member of a senior management team to listen and be listened to. The result reported was a time savings of 62%. This translated into 2,304 manager hours per year. (Time to Think, page 70). That is basically the equivalent of one person (or FTE). Think about what could be done with one additional person on your team!

What is listening? Listening is:

- Being curious about the other person

- Quieting your own mind chatter so you can be fully present with another person
- Creating a safe space for someone to explore
- Conveying value. You are important to me!
- Not about giving answers, but exploring possibilities
- Reflecting back, like a mirror, what you experienced from the person
- Really "getting" another person

And note there's a huge difference between hearing and listening:

- Hearing is an auditory process. Listening is an intentional process.
- Hearing is done with the ears. Listening involves all of the senses and the total being.
- Hearing includes words, details and information. Listening adds deeper layers.
- Hearing is to know about someone. Listening is knowing someone.
- Listening is a skill to be developed.

Coaches listen so closely the answers almost come out on their own. The ideal listening ratio is to be listening 80% of the time and responding 20% of the time. Someone once told me words comprise about 7% of what we communicate. In other words, most of our communication does not involve words. Coaches know this. That's why coaches listen at multiple levels. Here's a sampling of what a coach is listening for:

- Listen to what the other person is saying, as well as what they are not saying.
- Listen from deep within (gut-level listening).
- Listen to "get" the other person.
- Listen without judgment, criticism or agenda. You are creating a safe place for the person to share.
- Listen without thinking about what you will be saying next.
- Listen for values, frustrations, motivation and needs.
- Listen for the greatness in the person you are coaching.
- Listen for limiting beliefs and false assumptions. What does this person really believe the outcome or future will be?
- Listen for shoulds, oughts and musts. They are frequent indicators of obligation and guilt versus what the person really wants.

- Listen for the obvious. What is the other person not seeing or not aware of?

- Listen for the tone, pace, volume, inflection and frequently used words. Also, notice when these change.

- Listen for the larger context.

- Listen attentively to the end of the statements. Remember the old faucets with well water? You needed to let them run awhile before you got the good water. The best words often flow out last as well!

- Listen to your reactions as you listen.

To be able to listen at multiple levels, a coach must quiet their mind of any mind chatter or internal conversations. They must create a physical environment that promotes deep listening, by attend to the space and pace of life and by managing their scheduling and calendar. Coaches grow to be comfortable with silence — resisting the urge to fill the space. As a new coach, I recall a seasoned coach saying deep listening is similar to standing in a pool. In order to see the bottom clearly, you must be still — absolutely still.

Pause for a moment and consider your own potential barriers to deep listening. What are some steps you can take to address these challenges?

Here are some exercises to improve your listening:

- **Mute the TV.** Since most of what is communicated is nonverbal, why not mute the TV and have some fun trying to guess what's being communicated? To really test this ability, tape the TV show, watch it with the sound muted, and then watch it again with the sound playing.

- **Mirroring.** Pair up with a partner, with each person taking a turn to talk and to listen. When you're the listener, do your best to listen as if you were a mirror. Reflect back what you heard. Then ask: Did I get that right? Did I hear you correctly?

- **Record a conversation.** With the permission of the other person, record a conversation in which you intentionally attempted to listen deeply. Right after the conversation, write down what your deep listening revealed. Then, go back and listen to the recording of the conversation. What more did you hear? What had you missed?

- **Practice selective listening.** Decide for the next week that you are going to be selective in your listening and really listen for one specific element. For example, you might choose to identify the values you hear underneath people's words. Or you might listen only for signs of frustration, or for signs of greatness. Over the course of the week, pay attention to that one select area, training yourself to listen for this one item. Notice when you hear the item clearly — what circumstances made that possible in you and around you? What was going on in the times when it was challenging to hear the item?

Remember, great listeners hear with their:

- **Ears.** They listen to the spoken words, as well as tone, pace, pitch and inflection. They listen for the essence of what is being said.
- **Eyes.** Most of our communication is nonverbal. Great listeners notice body language of the one speaking.
- **Full body and being.** Gifted listeners notice how they are receiving the message. They pay attention to what is happening inside of them as they listen.

2. Powerful Questions

On my recent travels to deliver a coach training program, I heard a statement on the radio that stopped me cold: History changed when a single question changed; when we stopped asking, "How do we get to the water?" and started asking, "How do we get the water to us?"

What a radical shift for us as human beings!

My thoughts went immediately to how this relates to us as leaders and individuals in organizations. How would our teams and organizations change if we were to change our questions?

For example, here are some of the questions you might be asking now:

1. How do we get "them" to come to us?
2. How much longer can we afford this?
3. How do we get people to buy into this?

Boards and leaders literally spend hours on Question #1, but I'm thinking that if we changed that question, we could produce entirely different outcomes.

What if we asked, "How can we go to them?" Or we could ask, "How can we have a positive impact on our customers?"

Question #2 suggests scarcity thinking—focusing on what's lacking instead of what's abundant. What if we ask, "What more can we do with the resources we have?" What if we look at, "How can we develop the people we have so they can make a bigger contribution and everyone wins?"

In Question #3, it sounds like we're trying to cajole or even manipulate people into doing something they don't really want to do. What if we ask, "What can we do to make the greatest impact, and how can we garner support? People are happy to invest time, energy and resources when it impacts the vision and others positively.

I invite you to listen for the questions you and your team and/or organization are asking. Are they limiting, like our examples above, or are they powerful? And what's the difference?

One of a coach's greatest tools is powerful questions. Powerful questions are usually open-ended, leaving room for contemplation and reflection, instead of being limited to yes or no or specific choices. Powerful questions promote the exploration of new possibilities and stimulate creativity. They place the individual or group in a place of responsibility. They empower individuals and groups to consider what is right for them.

Powerful questions open us to possibilities beyond the reality that's in front of us today, stretching us into the territory of our visions to ask, "What is the opportunity for us this situation?"

Limiting questions, on the other hand, might not be questions at all. They may only be thinly masking a statement of blame, obligation of guilt, e.g., "Why did you do it that way?"

Here are a few powerful questions for consideration:

- How could you make better use of your personal strengths?
- How could you make better use of the strengths of your team and/or organization?
- What kind of leader would you be if you were driven by passion?
- Which of your roles could someone else be doing, and probably better than you?
- What's the worst thing that could happen if you did less?

What makes a question powerful? Powerful questions are:

- **Directly connected to deep listening, enabling the coach to craft the most effective question.** Early on in my coaching I believed there was only one right question and I would even equip myself with a long list of questions that I could scan while coaching. What I quickly discovered was that the most powerful questions were created in the moment and the power of the question was directly related to my ability to listen deeply.

- **Brief.** They get right to the point. It can be difficult to resist adding an explanation or another question instead of just waiting for the person to respond.

- **Free of any hidden agenda.** They are not leading or suggestive. In the coaching profession we refer to leading questions as "que-ggestions." Powerful questions help the person or group being coached to move further along the path of discovery.

- **Usually open-ended, promoting further conversation.** For the most part, yes/no questions usually result in a yes/no response, which force an end to the conversation and enable either/or thinking. Powerful questions promote both/and thinking, opening up the coachee to a fuller range of possibilities.

- **Clarifying.** They help clarify and slow down automatic responses and thinking. Coaching clients have told me time and time again that they appreciate how coaching creates the opportunity for them to step aside — push the pause button — and discern what they really want.

- **Perspective-shifting.** Powerful questions invite us to walk across to the other side of the room and look at the same thing from a different angle or perspective.

- **Benefits the one we are coaching.** Remember that the coach is not the expert, and does not have to figure anything out or come up with solutions. Therefore, our questions must be designed to help the coachee discover and develop their own perspective and wisdom about the situation.

Types of powerful questions

Questions that help the person gain perspective and understanding:

- What's the truth about this situation?
- Who do you remind yourself of?
- What keeps you up at night?
- Is there anything else that would be important for me to know?

Questions that evoke discovery:

- What do you really, really want?
- What's perfect about this?
- What is the gift in this?
- What additional information do you need?

- How much is this costing you?
- Who can help you with this?

Questions that promote clarity and learning:

- What if things are as bad as you say they are?
- Where are you sabotaging yourself?
- What's the cost of not changing?
- What's next?
- What's past this issue?

Questions that call for action:

- What's possible today?
- How soon can you resolve this?
- Who do you know that's going through this?
- What does success look like?
- What's the first step? When will you take this step?

Consider the following quote:

> "People remember ... things they discover, learn and experience
> themselves. If you want someone to digest and remember something,
> ... ask him a question."
> — *Dorothy Leeds, Smart Questions*

At the beginning of this section on powerful questions, you read that history changed when a single question changed. Questions are a powerful tool at our disposal. A powerful question, created out of deep listening, can change everything. Change the questions, change your organization.

Below are exercises, strategies and examples to further develop your understanding and use of powerful questions:

- **Scenario #1:** Your leadership team has been unable to take action on something decided months ago. Your team seems stuck on this issue. What powerful questions could you ask?

- **Scenario #2:** You are designing a new service offering and are looking for a specific response from key stakeholders. What powerful questions could you ask?

- **Scenario #3:** You are meeting with a team who is struggling to work together effectively. The team members have a fairly healthy relationship with each other but are stuck on this one issue. Several team members are blaming each other. What powerful questions could you ask this team?

Top 10 Questions

1. On a scale of 1 to 10, how would you rate...?
2. What's the payoff of not taking action?
3. What's the truth about this situation?
4. What's your vision?
5. What's past this?
6. What keeps getting in the way?
7. What's the simplest solution?
8. Who can help you with this?
9. What do you think about when you're lost in thought?
10. What do you really, REALLY want?

Some people collect stamps, coins or spoons—I collect questions. I'm positively intrigued by questions. For more of my favorite questions, please see Appendix A at the end of the book.

Jump start your next meeting with powerful questions

A common complaint I hear from leaders is about poor discussion and input from team members: "How do we get people to share their ideas and comments at our meetings? We even send out the agenda ahead of time and no one seems prepared to discuss things."

Let me offer a simple change that often jumpstarts the discussion. Instead of creating an agenda with topics to discuss, develop a couple of questions from your original agenda that start people thinking. For example:

Original agenda:

1. Financial Update
2. Leadership Team Report
3. Team Metrics Update
4. Other

Revised agenda with questions:

1. What are some ways to generate additional revenue during our slow summer months?
2. We need to develop a new hiring and retention strategy. Who has some thoughts to share on this topic?
3. We have a trend over the last three months of not achieving our customer satisfaction metric. What is our next step?

3. Artful Language

Many of us grew up hearing the statement "sticks and stones may break my bones, but words can never harm me." Nothing could be further from the truth!

Our words matter! Our language can provide a platform that motivates someone forward to peak performance, the perfect career or becoming a better leader. At the same time, our language can reinforce doubts and limiting beliefs—dashing hopes and dreams. Think of language like a scalpel; in the hands of the skillful and altruistic, it can be invaluable, while in the hand of the reckless or malicious, it can have devastating effects. Language is like the paintbrush in a coach's hand; it is the playground for our meaningful work.

Let's check out four pieces of equipment on the coach's playground:

*   Our actual words.
*   Matching of words.
*   Distinctions.
*   Acknowledgement.

Our Actual Words

Ask yourself—how are my chosen words resonating with the other person? In coaching, we often refer to this as how something "lands." Are my actual words fostering a safe and inviting environment that encourages the other person to go deeper below the surface to the core issues? Or, is the other person so busy dodging and ducking the zingers you're hurling at them they can only say "ouch!"

In our day-to-day conversations, words often contain assumptions, presuppositions, judgments, manipulation and suggestions. In coaching conversations, we intentionally choose words that are neutral, non-manipulative and free of any agenda. Our tone of voice is equally important. The same word with a different tone can be received entirely differently.

The Matching of Words and Language

Coaches notice the words and phrases of the other person. When appropriate, a coach will match their words and phrases with the person they are coaching and introduce new words or phrases. Coaches also pay attention to the pace and pattern of the other person's language. For example, when asked a question, introverts tend to process first and then talk, while extroverts tend to process by talking to arrive at an answer. The seasoned coach will sometimes match the other person to convey a feeling of acceptance; other times he or she will intentionally change up the pace and pattern to get the coachee's attention and make a point.

The coach is also listening for words that help the other person learn, describe their values and define their reality. These can be very useful in facilitating a shift. Often these are popular words or phrases from current or past culture. They can include TV, movies, music, metaphors, stories and quotes.

Examples of metaphors:

- The fruit doesn't fall far from the tree.
- Breaking the glass ceiling.
- Swimming in a sea of choices.
- Drinking from a firehose.
- Pulling yourself up by your bootstraps.
- It sounds like you're on a see-saw.
- It doesn't work to leap a 20-foot chasm in two 10-foot jumps. (American proverb)

Examples of stories:

- The "Emperor's New Clothes" and the importance of truth-telling.
- Forrest Gump's "Life is like a box of chocolates."
- Humpty Dumpty's lesson that some things in life can never be put back together again.

Examples of quotes:

- "And the day came when the risk to remain tight in a bud was more painful than the risk it took to blossom." —*Anais Nin*
- "It is a terrible thing to look over your shoulder when leading and find no one there." —*Franklin Delano Roosevelt*
- "Most leaders don't need to learn what to do. They need to learn what to stop." —*Peter Drucker*

Examples from popular media culture include:

- The song "Don't Worry, Be Happy."
- "You're fired!" from Donald Trump's TV show *The Apprentice*.
- The TV show *Survivor* and the phrase "getting voted off the island."
- A place "where everybody knows your name," as revered in the theme song of the long-running TV show *Cheers*.

Distinctions

Distinctions are two words or phrases that are close in meaning, yet convey subtle differences. Those subtle differences create a new awareness that is instrumental in propelling the individual forward.

Consider the following distinction and the subtle, yet huge, shift it creates—definition by obstacles versus definition by opportunities:

- To define yourself by obstacles means you are defining who you are and the decisions you make based on the challenges you are facing. A life defined by obstacles is reactive. It is moving away from someone or something.
- To define yourself by opportunities means you define who you are and base your decisions on your opportunities. It's not that you're ignoring the obstacles, you've just decided to keep your sights on the bigger picture—your vision. It is moving toward someone or something and is usually proactive.

Additional distinctions:

- Perfection versus excellence.
- Adding more versus adding value.
- Living by default versus living by design.
- Working hard versus producing results.
- Either/or versus both/and.
- Prioritizing what's on your schedule versus scheduling your priorities.
- Doing powerfully effective things versus being powerfully effective.
- Planning versus preparing.

Distinctions are a much more subtle version of the "shifts" that often occur when a coachee takes the awareness created in the coaching session and puts it into action. Below are five shifts coaches might want to consider to move forward effectively as a coach:

- From diagnosing to developing
- From doing to empowering
- From telling to exploring
- From mindlessness to mindfulness
- From excellence to effectiveness

Acknowledgment

Most people, when asked to create a list of their weaknesses and also a list of their strengths, find it easier to list their weaknesses. Why? Many people assume if I can just fix my weaknesses or if I could only correct what's wrong with me, eventually I will be great!

Consider the following: The average person, on any given day, has between 12,000 and 50,000 thoughts. By the age of eight, most of those thoughts are negative thoughts (e.g., I'm not good enough. I can't do it. What's wrong with me?). Your organization and, in fact, the entire world is made up of people who already speak to themselves with judgment and disapproval.

Acknowledgment creates an environment of acceptance and safety. When people feel safe and accepted, they are more likely to be curious and explore new things.

> "We are not expected to be who we are not. We are expected to be who we are."
> *(Living Your Strengths, by Albert L. Winseman, Donald O. Clifton and Curt Liesveld, Page 10).*

I mentioned Ben Zander earlier; he understands the importance of acknowledgment. When he uses his "A" approach in class, he is not only focusing on the person his students will become but he is also acknowledging the greatness within his students and is inviting them to live into that greatness.

Effective organizations will be about giving an "A" — genuinely tapping into people's greatness. Imagine if organizations were known for giving "A's," instead of judgment. Or, if the focus of organizations shifted from what they are not to who they are, as well as who they are becoming, what shifts would occur? How different would organizations be if leaders regularly focused on acknowledging the strengths of employees? How different would your organization be if leaders regularly focused on acknowledging the strengths of employees? How different would you be?

Remember Nancy Kline and her book *Time to Think* (pages 62-64)? We read about how society teaches us to be positive is to be naïve and vulnerable, whereas to be critical is to be informed, buttressed and sophisticated. Many people are taught that to be appreciated is a slippery slope towards gross immodesty. It's as if, when you hear something nice about yourself and don't reject it instantly, you will, presto, turn into an out-of-control egomaniac. This is ridiculous.

Actually, change takes place best in a large context of genuine praise, Kline asserts. Appreciation (what we are calling acknowledgment) is important not because it feels good or is nice, but because it helps people think for themselves on the cutting edge of an issue. We should aim for a 5:1 ratio of appreciation to criticism. Being appreciated increases your intelligence and helps you think better.

4. Action and Accountability

When we began exploring action and accountability, a participant at a coach training event declared, "Finally, the good stuff!" When I asked what he meant he said that everything we had discussed up until now, while helpful information, didn't really matter unless action happened. In many respects, he was right. One of the primary reasons a person or a group decides to work with a coach is that they want to take action and reach their goals.

Action and forward progress are indeed the good stuff. There are three components to action and accountability:

1. Brainstorming
2. Designing the action
3. Follow through

It's really tempting at this point in the coaching process to jump right in and design an action plan. I want you to resist that urge and instead take a few more moments to brainstorm. Why am I suggesting this? Our coachee's tendency is going to be to take similar action steps as before, if not the same exact actions. The trouble is those same action steps are going to generate the same outcomes. The reason this person or group is in coaching is to get different results! A quote on my office wall reminds me of this principle:

Nothing changes, if nothing changes.

Brainstorming

Brainstorming helps someone see the same thing differently. Brainstorming enables the individual to discover for themselves different perspectives and possibilities. This involves distinguishing between fact, perception and interpretation, as well as gaining clarity and defining success.

A great example of brainstorming occurred during an episode of the TV sitcom "Seinfeld," featuring Jerry's friend George Costanza. George was one of those people who couldn't do anything right. He was in his 30s, he still lived at home, and he had no job or relationship and was losing the rest of his hair. And he was often thought of as being unattractive.

And then George Costanza had a major epiphany. George said something like this: "Jerry, it's very clear to me that my life is the opposite of everything I want it to be. From now on I'm going to do the opposite."

Do you remember what happened when George did the opposite? Things turned out very well because George was willing to look at things entirely differently and step out of his comfort zone.

I want those I coach to have those kinds of epiphanies when we brainstorm together before creating an action plan. I usually start by asking them to identify a next step—what they would usually do next. Then, I ask them to set that action aside for the moment and come up with 50 other possible actions. Most laugh at this request. Many are speechless. I restate my request and give them some prompts, such as:

- What's the most outrageous step you could take?
- What's the simplest next step?
- Who could help you generate more ideas for next steps?
- What possibilities have you repeatedly dismissed?

Years ago I coached a leader about casting the vision for his organization. His usual method of vision-casting was to present a compelling vision at the beginning of each new year. Upon inquiry he acknowledged this method stirred people for a couple of days but produced no real progress. I then asked him to set that action step aside and requested over the next two weeks that he identify 50 other ways to cast vision. He repeatedly stated he didn't know any others, and I repeatedly requested he come up with his list.

Two weeks later he came back with a list of 50 ways to catch the vision. Here's how he did it: The day after our previous coaching session, he went to his leadership team and kiddingly told the team about the outrageous request his coach had made of him—50 ways to cast the vision. One of his leadership team members jokingly referred to the rock song "50 Ways to Leave Your Lover" and another team member laughingly said we could put together a song called "50 Ways to Cast Our Vision" and present it to our employees at our annual sales meeting. In the following moments, with the help of his leadership team, he started considering 50 other ways to cast vision. Now he was ready to design the action plan!

Designing the Action

Within the context of brainstorming, a plan begins to emerge. The plan includes next steps that are attainable, measurable, specific, and have target dates. In most cases the plan addresses both what you need to do and who you need to become in order to reach your goal. Commitment, like the "50 ways to cast our vision," usually comes naturally and effortlessly

Techniques useful for designing the action include:

- **Baby steps.** Sometimes people are immobilized with all that needs to happen. Breaking the action steps into smaller steps can help them begin taking action.
- **Backward planning.** Begin at the end (the goal) and then move backward and develop steps to get to the goal.
- **Acknowledging.** Recognizing what has been accomplished.
- **Creating structure.** Identifying what and who will keep the client focused on the task at hand.
- **Strategizing.** Considering what might derail progress and design action steps in advance.
- **Anchoring.** Regularly reminding the person or group of the importance of what they are doing and where they are in the plan.
- **"Blitz Days."** Helping them carve out solid blocks of time to tackle everything that is getting in the way or needs to be done to stay on task.
- **Identify daily action.** These help create daily movement and momentum.

Sometimes formulas can be helpful. Consider the G.R.O.W. Model:

G	Goal	What's the goal?
R	(Current) Reality	How are we doing?
O	Opportunities	What are our current opportunities?
W	What	What's the next step?

Follow Through

In an ongoing coaching relationship, you are checking in regarding ongoing progress and course corrections. In most cases, I coach people twice a month—that's two times every month for us to follow through. I usually begin each coaching session with questions like these:

- What's happened since the last time we met?
- What didn't happen that you really intended to happen?
- What got in the way? What were the challenges?
- What will you report back to me the next time we meet, regarding this action?
- What do you want to focus on today?

Notice that the accountability is palatable as we define completion. There is no judgment or shame involved. There is no guilt or manipulation. This ongoing accountability is a natural part of the coaching relationship. A leader once stated that accountability is really about "goaltending."

5. The Coaching Relationship

In real estate, the three most important things are: location, location and location. It can also be stated that, in coaching, the three most important things are: relating, relating and relating. The coaching relationship is the vehicle of change and transformation.

One way to view the coaching relationship is as a dance. Let's use the example of the great dance couple Fred Astaire and Ginger Rogers to describe the dance of the coaching relationship. Consider Fred Astaire as the coachee and Ginger Rogers the coach. Notice that Ginger did everything Fred did (only backwards and in high heels!) but that she takes her lead from Fred.

Let's stay with the dance of coaching to further understand the unique and skillful way in which a coach relates. Fred and Ginger developed a safety and trust that let them draw close to each other. A level of intimacy was present, yet never violated. This allowed them to really "get" each other and almost anticipate each other's moves. Coaches are able to be totally spontaneous, while also being fully present and in the moment. This total spontaneity involves a knowing beyond what is typically, or rationally, known and observed. It's similar to the athlete who can anticipate where the ball will be thrown, before it's thrown.

New coaches often ask, "How do you further develop coaching presence—your own deeper level of knowing?" There are no shortcuts to develop a deeper level of knowing. It all begins with deep listening. Practice listening, and then practice again and again. Develop and use powerful questions, and make artful choices with your language. Here are some additional tools that have helped others:

- **Note-taking.** The act of writing helps many go deeper. Jot down what you're noticing in the coaching session. Remember, deep listening uses the eyes, as well as the ears. The challenge of note-taking is to take notes in such as way it enhances rather than interferes with your deep listening.

- **Self-care.** It's hard to go deeper when you're barely managing life on the surface. Like they tell us on airplanes—place the mask on yourself first and then your children. Similarly, take care of yourself first before you attempt to assist others.

- **Review your coaching.** Make a recording of a coaching session and then review it. Then take it one step further and ask your mentor-coach to review it and give you feedback, specifically about your coaching presence.

- **Quiet your mind.** Intentionally quiet yourself before and after a coaching session. Show up with a clean frame of reference and a quiet mind. Then spend time reflecting after the session on what worked and what you might do differently the next time you coach.

- **Risk.** Share your hunches, inklings or gut feelings. Preface your hunch by saying something like "I'd like to go out on a skinny branch for a moment with you. I could be completely wrong, but here's what I'm wondering (or noticing)…"

- **Listen from the heart versus the head (or vice versa).** Be intentional in shifting from intellect to intuition. Request that the person you are coaching also get out of their head and listen from the heart. Ask them "What are you feeling in your body right now? What might your body be trying to tell you?"

Let's go back to Fred and Ginger for another unique component of the coaching relationship. Notice that Fred and Ginger aren't trying to correct or judge each other's steps while they dance. There is a mutual respect for the other's level of skills and competence. They each have their unique experience, strength and gifts. And the way they relate to each other brings out the best in the other. On the dance floor they are tapped into each other's strengths.

In your day-to-day work and personal life, practice intentionally listening and looking for greatness. At first you'll probably notice how much easier it is to diagnose and how frequently you miss the opportunities to develop others. Be kind to yourself—most of today's leaders, paid and unpaid, have been formally and informally trained to diagnose problems, not necessarily to develop others. Over time you'll begin to notice those "development" moments.

Next, begin to tell others what you notice about their strengths and gifts. They may dismiss it or disqualify it. Keep telling them anyway, because what's important is the shift you're making in how you relate to them—as a partner in their success. Eventually, like Fred and Ginger, you'll be tapping into the strengths of others with ease and grace. And you'll also notice your new way of relating will be an attractive magnet for drawing people to you and your team or organization.

A positive coaching relationship will increase your coachee's likelihood of success. Since they relate well to you, they are more likely to explore further and take bigger steps, plus they will stick with their plan of action longer.

6. The Coaching Agreement

As leaders, we often find ourselves saying, "If you need something from me, please tell me. If I don't know what you need or want, I can only guess at what you need and want. I am not a mind reader."

The same is true of coaches—we aren't mind readers—that's why we have a coaching agreement. A coaching agreement is a way to define the requirements and process behind the coaching relationship. The coaching agreement takes most of the guesswork out of coaching and makes it possible for the coach to follow the coachee—not the other way around.

While newer coaches see the coaching agreement as a once-and-done process, masterful coaches understand the ongoing nature of the coaching agreement. There are three parts to the coaching agreement:

- The initial agreement
- The ongoing agreement
- The evaluation process

The initial coaching agreement includes:

- Defining the terms of the coaching relationship in writing; for example, fees, schedule, responsibilities, and expectations of the coach and coachee. If you are an internal coach we still recommend you have a coaching agreement that outlines expectations.
- Articulating what coaching is and isn't.
- Discerning whether or not the coach and coachee are a good match.
- Clarifying the needs of the coachee and why they want to work with a coach. I like to ask "What do you want to be able to say three months from now that you cannot say today?" This helps both the coach and coachee gain clarity about the desired outcome.

The ongoing coaching agreement includes:

- Helping the coachee clarify what they want to focus on in each particular coaching session, as well as what they want to take away.

- Further clarifying and exploring what the coachee is taking away from the coaching session.

- Holding side-by-side the initial desired outcomes and goals that brought them to coaching and the current focus/take-away. Because coaching is focused on discovery and not outcomes, new insights and perspectives need to be continually integrated into the coaching agreement.

The third component of the coaching agreement is the evaluation process. This frequently includes course corrections, or may also involve a dramatic shift in the overall desired outcome. I frequently ask questions such as:

- How are we doing?

- Based on our coaching to date, what's your ongoing, developing vision?

- On a scale of 1-10, rate the overall progress you've made. What is needed to take it up several levels?

- What more do I need to know about you, your learning preferences, or background to accelerate your progress/performance?

- Where is self-sabotage showing up?

- What additional supports are needed?

- What will you report back to me the next time we meet?

A frequent mistake new coaches make is in moving through the coaching agreement quickly—in as little as two to five minutes. The clearer the coachee and coach are with the agreement, the better the outcome. It's not unusual to spend the bulk of a coaching session on this area—15-20 minutes. Here are questions and statements that help coachees and their coaches fine-tune the coaching agreement and evaluate the coaching process:

- **Tell me more.** Because people are so busy, they rarely have time to think and talk. It's extremely beneficial to intentionally provide space for people to say more. Time and time again we hear coachees extol the benefits of "getting things out."

- **What is the one thing I need to hear in order to best coach you?** This helps the coachee get laser-focused and selective about sharing only what's absolutely critical to their overall progress.

- **Taking into account all that's on your plate right now, is this topic/ issue the most important one (and if not, what is)?** Similarly, this question helps the coachee hone in on the topics and issues that will contribute the most to their overall success and satisfaction.

This coaching scenario will help you to further understand the coaching agreement:

> Steve is the founder and senior leader of a rapidly growing company. He currently has 22 full-time employees on his team. He frequently describes his team as a family. It's not unusual for Steve to "go the extra mile" and bend the rules for individual members of his team, because he considers them to be his family. He finds it difficult to reprimand them and to implement performance plans, let alone even consider firing anyone, because he really views his staff as family and is concerned with their well-being.
>
> Steve's vision is to grow into a global organization. He believes he can do this within the next three to five years. In addition to implementing this global vision, he would also like to spend less time at work and enjoy life more. His big dream is to take six weeks off next summer and tour Europe with his family, and let his leadership team run the company in his absence.
>
> Steve has created a strategic plan and action steps to move towards his goal. He's making moderate progress. He is becoming very aware that his current leadership team is slowing things down. He is also frustrated his "company family" doesn't share the enthusiasm for his vision. Steve hired a coach to help him implement his global plan, with a special emphasis on how he can empower and equip the leadership team to lead the implementation of the plan.
>
> During a recent coaching session, Steve expressed frustration about his vision and his "company family," and then made the following statement about himself: "Maybe I'm the one that's holding back this vision. It feels like all the pieces are there, but maybe there's something that needs to change about me."

In your words, describe the focus of this coaching relationship (as may have been determined in the initial coaching agreement).

What are Steve's new discoveries? What other new discoveries do you see ahead for Steve?

In what ways will these new discoveries impact the coaching agreement?

In what ways will the coaching agreement remain the same?

After hearing Steve state, "Maybe I'm the one that's holding us back," how would you coach Steve?

7. Creating New Awareness

Brainstorming is an excellent way to explore new ways of doing things. Creating awareness takes it one step further and explores new ways of being, as well as doing. It's like working the plates deep within the earth, resulting in major shifts and changes. Let me give you several examples:

- Consider this statement from one leader I coached: "I'm an introvert and everyone knows that introverts aren't good leaders." No amount of doing would result in any lasting change. This individual needed to go down deep and create a new awareness of his strengths.

- Consider the leadership team that fizzled out partway through a visioning process. The consultant tried everything to get them moving and then finally inquired what was happening. After what seemed like an eternity of silence, one of the key leaders finally responded that they had gotten to this point on two previous occasions within the past five years and, in each instance, their leader had moved on before the projects were completed. No sooner had the words been spoken when the leadership team had a major "aha." They embraced their new awareness and began moving forward.

- Consider the awareness that launched my career as a full-time coach. As a part-time coach, my business growth was slowed by the belief that "he is just a pastor" and no one would hire a pastor as their coach. When my coach helped me verbalize this limiting belief, it created an awareness of the truth that my ideal clients will seek me out and hire me precisely because I am a pastor.

Creating new awareness is like raising the blinds and letting in the light of additional information, perspective and intention. New awareness is fostered when:

- Curiosity is encouraged.
- Clarifying questions are raised.
- Beliefs and assumptions are articulated and verified.
- You intentionally consider a different perspective.
- You are open to other ways of viewing and interpreting the same situation.

How does the coach facilitate new awareness?

- **Contextual listening.** The coach considers and explores the various contexts of the person being coached (e.g., the bigger picture, the total person, previous experiences, and the values of the person).
- **Missing pieces.** The coach helps individuals and groups see and say what they can't quite see or say. Because the coach is listening on multiple levels, the coach hears underlying values, motivation, greatness, frustration, etc. Simply being a mirror and holding up for the other what we're observing creates new awareness.
- **Drilling down.** Similar to the layers of an onion, the coaching process peels away the layers and gets to the core issues.
- **Listening for clues.** A coachee is always offering clues about themselves. R.D. Lang wrote, "The range of what we think and do is limited by what we fail to notice. And because we fail to notice that we fail to notice, there is little we can do to change; until we notice how failing to notice shapes our thoughts and deed."

    Here are some powerful questions that will uncover important clues:

    - What kind of problems and crises do you keep attracting?
    - What do you keep doing that limits your success?
    - What thoughts are repeatedly playing in your head?

Eliminating Limiting Beliefs and False Assumptions

One of the most powerful ways of creating awareness in a coaching relationship is to help the coachee identify and transform their limiting beliefs and false assumptions.

Use the following list to see if you recognize some of your own:

- I have to have all the answers.
- I have no choice.
- I have no power.
- I cannot lead.
- Change is always difficult.
- It isn't possible.
- What doesn't kill you makes you stronger.
- Peace is always better than honesty.

List three of your limiting beliefs:

1. _____

2. _____

3. _____

List three of your false assumptions:

1. _____

2. _____

3. _____

Limiting beliefs and false assumptions can be very simple, yet very harmful. In her book *Time to Think,* Nancy Kline offers a simple yet profound method of dealing with limiting beliefs and false assumptions. One of her tips is to help your coachee articulate the "positive opposite" of their limiting belief or false assumption. This is often a difficult task for an individual or team to do, but press them to articulate the positive opposite of their bedrock assumption. Once articulated, ask them to write it down and say it several times.

8. Direct Communication

If you spend time with a seasoned coach, you will notice the masterful way that they communicate. For example, you will almost never hear a masterful coach ramble. Most seasoned coaches are clear, concise and laser-like with their words, offering one question or statement at a time.

Another characteristic is their comfort with silence. There is no attempt to idly fill space; rather, an appropriate use of silence and pauses is demonstrated.

And coaches tell the truth. They don't hold back on whatever needs to be said, even if it isn't always the nicest thing to hear or the most comfortable thing to say.

Seasoned coaches are direct in their communication, using language that will have the greatest positive impact on the person being coached. Four of the most important direct communication techniques are:

- Interrupting
- Advising
- Directing
- Messaging

Interrupting

Most of us have experienced interruptions as distracting or annoying, but effective interrupting is truly an art. As a coaching skill, masterful interrupting holds great benefit for the coachee, bringing them back on task, or helping them to "bottom-line" (get to the point).

Coaches interrupt within an environment of trust and intimacy, one in which the coachee trusts the skill of the coach and knows the coach has their best interest in mind. Interrupting can stem from deep listening, as a means of getting at something even deeper that needs to be said. Interrupting is a platform from which to catapult the coachee forward.

During my initial coaching sessions with new coachees, part of the initial agreement is for them to give me permission to interrupt them, when appropriate. Having this conversation on the front end of the coaching experience helps the coachee expect the interruptions and see them in a positive light.

When is it appropriate to interrupt someone you are coaching?

Here are several ways I may interrupt someone while coaching:

- Say their name and ask for permission; e.g., "(Name), may I interrupt you?"
- Break in with "Let's push the pause button for a moment," or "I'd like to step in for a moment."
- Bottom-line it for them, e.g.; "(Name), here's what I'm hearing..."

Advising

One of the myths of coaching is that coaches never give advice. That's a myth? Let me explain. First and foremost the coach wants to tap into the expertise of the one they are coaching. Got it! And, there are also times when the coach has expertise and experiences that can have a positive impact on the forward progress of the coachee. During a workshop at an International Coach Federation Conference, the presenter stated that #7 on the top 10 list of what people want in a coach is advice. The qualifiers are they want advice from their coach when appropriate and when asked for.

The problem with giving advice is most people offer advice in ways that are disempowering of others. They need to unlearn how to give advice and then re-learn how to advise. I suggest newer coaches completely refrain from offering advice, at least for a time. Once they have learned how to effectively coach without giving advice, they can begin incorporating advice-giving into their coaching when appropriate and when asked for.

Consider the following tips when offering advice:

- Listen deeply. Hear all the person has to say.
- Don't offer advice until you have thought through how the advice may be misheard.
- Don't give advice until you have heard all the facts.
- Don't forget it's ONLY ADVICE; it's not a cure for global warming.
- Phrasing examples:
  - Here's what I've seen work. Tell me if it sounds like it's worth experimenting with.
  - That's a tough one. Here's what I advised another person and this is what happened.

Directing

Directing is a technique for refocusing or steering the person or group back toward their goals. This is useful for the coachee who frequently goes off on tangents or easily loses sight of the big picture.

Examples of directing:

- Hold that thought and let's talk about...
- For the past several weeks we've been focusing on ABC. Is it time to move on to XYZ?
- Congratulations. Let's move on.

Messaging

Messaging is a "truth" that, if heard, will help the other person to understand and act more quickly. It is a "blending" of acknowledging and tapping into the person's greatness.

Examples of messaging include:

- Tell them who they are. "You are someone who is... "
- Endorse what they have accomplished. "Wow. Look what you've accomplished. Congratulations."
- Tell them what's next. "You probably need to start focusing on ABC, since you've moved past XYZ."
- Tell them what you want for them. "What I want for you is..."

Chapter Three
A Five-Step Coaching Model

Now that you have the building blocks of coaching skills and techniques, it's time to put them together. The following coaching model will provide a framework you can come back to over and over again as your skills progress and you coach more diverse and interesting people and situations

Solid coaching, like a solid house, has a:

Foundation

- Listen
- Evoke

Supportive Frame

- Clarify
- Brainstorm

Strong covering

- Support

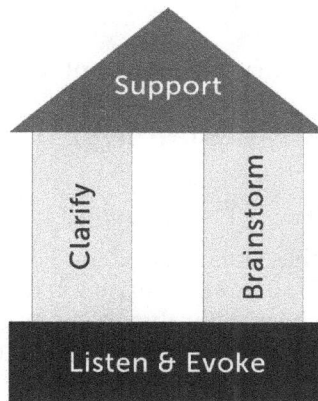

The eight common coaching scenarios we will address include:

Laying the foundation

Step 1: Listen

The goal as a coach is to listen so closely to your client the answers come out. The ideal ratio is you are listening 80% of the time and responding 20% of the time. It is absolutely critical that the client feel fully understood. Listen deeply by using these suggestions:

- Listen not just with your ears, but with your eyes and your whole being ("gut-level" listening).
- Listen to the tone, inflection, rate and pitch.
- Listen not just to what's said, but to what's not said.
- Pay particular attention to the last thing that is said.

- Listen without judgment, criticism or agenda.
- Listen without thinking about what you will be saying next.

Step 2: Evoke

Prompt the coachee to say more. Evoking is like opening the tap. You are attempting to get beyond the surface and move to the source of the issue.

Examples of evocative responses:

- Hmmmm.
- What else do you want to say about this?
- Tell me more.
- Is there anything else you want me to know?

Propping up the supports

Step 3: Clarify

Once the coachee has shared and has actively engaged with you, it's important to respond and clarify what is being said. This offers the client an opportunity to hear what they have just verbalized from a slightly different perspective. It also ensures you and the client are on the same page.

Examples of clarifying techniques:

- I heard you say… (mirroring)
- I sense that… (paraphrasing or reflecting back)
- Is this what you mean? (verifying)
- On a scale of I to I0 how committed are you to this? I=not important, I0=important (rating)
- Number these things based on which is most important to you 1=least important, 10=most important (ranking

Step 4: Brainstorm

Once there is clarity about the topic at hand, you and the coachee can now begin to go below the surface and further discuss the issue. Questions are central to the coaching process, and a more complete list of questions is found at the end of this book.

A few examples of questions include:

- What are the options/opportunities here? Let's list them all.
- What's the simplest solution? What's the craziest solution?
- What's the payoff of NOT dealing with this?
- What's stopping you?
- What do you want to be able to say about this situation three months from now that you can't say today?
- What do you really, REALLY want?

Providing a cover

Step 5: Support

Action is central to the coaching experience. Supporting the coachee to design an action step helps move the coachee forward, closing the gap between where they currently are and where they want to be.

A typical coaching conversation might end like this:

- Based on our conversation today, what action would you like to take? And when will it be completed?
- What do you want to report back to me at our next coaching session?
- What will bring you closer to your goal?
- What will you need to be able to focus on this next week?
- What will get in the way?
- Who can help you with this?

In subsequent coaching sessions, you'll follow up by asking questions such as:

- What did you accomplish?
- What didn't you accomplish that you said you would?
- What got in the way?
- What's next?

Chapter Four
Coaching Scenarios

Here are several coaching scenarios you can use to practice applying your coaching techniques and skills, within the framework of this coaching model. Answer each question in writing.

Case #1: Dave

Dave was promoted to Senior Manager of his current team six months ago. This is his first experience in a more senior role, and he is leading others who used to be his peers. Prior to this assignment he spent three years as a Benefits Supervisor and thoroughly loved it. Dave has a lot of energy for his new role. The team he is currently leading has lost a few team members due to a recent reduction in force (RIF) and when Dave came on as the leader he was the third leader in the last two years.

Dave's supervisor has stated on numerous occasions that building the team and achieving departmental metrics is to be Dave's top priority. Dave regularly invests his time and energy in areas other than team development and metrics achievement. Dave has also said on several occasions, "I am not sure I am a right fit for this new role." He supports this statement with numerous assessment tools he has recently taken. One example is that his Myers-Briggs Type Indicator revealed he is an introvert. Dave has stated repeatedly introverts aren't good leaders, much less at developing teams. This supports Dave's belief he's not a good leader. Dave's supervisor has requested he hire a coach to help him develop his leadership capability.

What are the key issues Dave is addressing?

What requests would you make of him?

How would you coach him?

What, if any, tools or resources would you use?

Case #2: John

John is in his second year as CEO of a well-established leadership team (most have been in their position for 10+ years), where little has changed in the organization or on the leadership team. Seven years ago, this organization entered a period of rapid growth on a global level. This growth occurred in both products and services as well as employees. Overnight, the organization grew by 50% and revenue skyrocketed. This required the organization to invest in research and real estate and required they move forward at an increasingly rapid rate to keep up with customer demands, competitors who were "nipping at their heels," and the every growing needs of a global employee base. Between melding company culture and global culture as well as increased customer demand, this organization found themselves at a critical point in their existence in terms of meeting and exceeding multiple priorities.

In the last two years, there has been a steady decline in growth and a sharp decline in the last six months. John is receiving pressure to consolidate product lines and close certain locations, while at the same time others are lobbying him to increase research and development and focus on new global markets. John feels torn between both groups and, while he sees the validity in each of their arguments, he knows he needs to make a decision quickly. Several of John's colleagues have worked with a coach and had recommended coaching. John hired a coach because he was at a complete loss as how to lead this organization through this time of great stress and change. John's first words to his coach were: "Business School didn't prepare me for anything like this. Help. What do I do?"

What are the key issues that John is addressing?

What requests would you make of him?

How would you coach him?

What, if any, tools or resources would you use?

Case #3: Kim

Kim fast tracked into an HR leadership position in her mid-thirties. She was very successful in two earlier careers, both in sales. Kim also has a PhD in Human Relations. Kim had been extremely active in her local SHRM group since starting her graduate degrees. Her decision to move into HR and get her advanced degrees in her late twenties felt like a natural next step for her. Kim regularly receives positive reviews from her superiors. They view Kim as a "high potential" and as such are providing her with developmental opportunities, such as additional training and senior leader mentors. Kim attributed much of her success in her earlier sales career to her work with a coach. She decided a coach would also benefit her as a new leader in HR.

During a recent coaching session, Kim stated: "I frequently feel overwhelmed. Being an HR professional is so different than being in Sales." A few minutes later she stated: "It's not supposed to be this hard, being in HR. I chose this field because I enjoy people, supporting their development and helping them and the organization move forward. Shouldn't it be easier? Shouldn't it come naturally to me? I felt energized during school and in my earlier HR positions. Now I rarely have time to support others or mentor my team, let alone develop myself. I am so focused on the "task" of HR that everything that attracted me to HR goes by the wayside. Did I make a mistake in moving to HR?"

What are the key issues that Kim is addressing?

What requests would you make of her?

How would you coach her?

What, if any, tools or resources would you use?

Chapter Five
Your Next Step

Congratulations! You Are Dangerous.

I'd like to conclude this book by offering you four simple words. The first word is—Congratulations! Reading this book is a solid first step in your development as a coach. This first step is something to be proud of and is a milestone to be acknowledged. I want to encourage you to put into daily practice the coaching skills and techniques you've just learned.

The three additional words I want to caution you with are—You Are Dangerous! Yes, you read that correctly. The danger is that leaders and individuals will stop after reading this book or after taking the introductory two-day training.

Coaching is not something I have just licensed you to dabble in, such as:

- Learning "just enough" of the coaching language to sprinkle through your consulting. The consulting is the same; the language is different.
- Picking and choosing a few things to try and then quickly abandoning them because "they" didn't work.
- Listening deeply and using powerful questioning for a time, then falling back into old patterns of fixing things and people.
- Settling for things getting a bit better, instead of striving to be the best coach and leader you can be.
- Seeing coaching as a set of skills, rather than as a radical and necessary change in your approach and perspective to ministry.

I challenge you not to dabble this way, but to embrace this paradigm shift and embrace a new way to empower others and yourself to forward movement and success!

To bring us back full circle to my introduction of this book, it is my vision that every leader have coach training in their professional toolkit. Thank you for reading this book and helping make my vision a reality!

Enjoy coaching!

Chapter Six
Additional Coaching Techniques and Strategies

We included in this text a number of exercises and techniques you can use in your coaching.

Focus Exercise

This exercise helps the individual gain clarity about their primary roles and responsibilities. Begin by writing your responses to each of these questions:

1. What are the things only you can do?
2. What are the things you and others can do?
3. What are the things you can do, but choose not to do?
4. What are the things you cannot do and never want to do?

Look over your answers and deepen your learning with these additional questions:

- How does what you have written compare with how you actually spend your time and energy?
- What would it take to spend the majority of your time doing what only you can do?
- Who do you need to be in order to make this a reality?

Identify the changes and adjustments necessary and take action now. Today.

Leadership Timetable

In order to respond to the challenges of leadership, leaders must make time for these priorities:

- **Rest:** Every good leader understands the importance of taking care of their physical body.
- **Results:** Make time for your main goals.
- **Response:** Make sure there is adequate time for follow-up and follow-through.
- **Refocus:** Schedule time for course corrections and fine-tuning.

Ask your coachees which of the four "Rs" they frequently forget. The final "R" is often the most overlooked. Then ask, "Which of these "Rs" would be of the greatest benefit to you and your movement forward?"

Self-Care

Self-Care includes four areas of rest. They include:

1. **Physical rest:** Make sure your body is getting adequate rest.
2. **Mind rest:** Enjoy some silence. Turn off the TV. Take a break from reading the depressing news in the paper. Just let your mind rest.
3. **Heart rest:** Caring for others and their needs can become exhausting. Take a short break and let others care for you. You'll be better able to care for others when you return.
4. **Soul rest:** Take time to experience your passions. Rest in the knowledge the world does not revolve around you or me!

When traveling by airplane, we're reminded in an emergency, those traveling with children are to put on their own oxygen mask first and then care for their children. A strong personal foundation is like putting on your oxygen mask first. You are then better able to care for and lead those around you.

Split Time versus Solid Time

A common challenge among coaching clients is getting things done, especially those items that only they can do. The To-Do list keeps growing. Feelings of guilt and inadequacy take root. The latest technological gismos are of no assistance. No matter what, there still aren't enough hours in the week to do all you want and need to do.

If you look more closely at your tasks and what they require, you can get past this bottleneck in no time. You see, some tasks require a solid block of time to be completed. These items often require a creative flow of thought or have a sequence/strategic process to them. Every time you stop and re-start a solid block project, you lose valuable time and momentum.

Split-time tasks, on the other hand, can be stopped and restarted with little to no loss of time or momentum. These kinds of tasks can be worked on when you discover a few extra minutes or when you're on auto-pilot.

Give this a try: Begin by identifying what you need to do in any given week. Then, for each task, decide if you need a "solid" block of time OR a "split" block of time.

You will be amazed at how this simple distinction will allow you to use your time so much more efficiently, and how much more quickly you will complete the tasks on your list.

Appendix A
A List of Powerful Questions

Top 10 Year-End Questions for You or Your Team

1. What have you accomplished this year? Be specific. Write it down. Schedule some time to celebrate this!

2. What have you learned this year? What skills did you pick up? What lessons?

3. What got in your way? Where will your work be next year? Be honest if it was you who got in the way.

4. Who contributed to your success? What can you do to recognize these members of your personal or professional team?

5. What mistakes did you make, and what did you learn from them? Writing these down is a good refresher for what not to do next year.

6. How was your work consistent with your values?

7. Where did you not take responsibility? Sometimes this is easier to see with a little distance from the actual event.

8. How did your performance rate? Give yourself a letter grade or a 1 to 10 score.

9. What do you need to let go of? Doing so can help you move much more lightly into the New Year.

10. What was missing for you this year? How can you incorporate it into next year?

Top 10 Questions for Leaders

1. What do you want to be able to say three years from now that you can't say today (about yourself or your organization)?

2. What are the possible next steps?

3. Who can help you with this?

4. What's the truth about now?

5. How do you handle failure?

6. What do you model?

7. How much of a people pleaser are you?

8. What do you need to say goodbye to in order to move forward?

9. On a scale of 1 to 10 how committed are you to taking action? (1= no commitment, 10=high commitment)

10. What's the payoff of not taking action?

Val's Favorite Questions

1. What's next?
2. What do you want?
3. What are you afraid of?
4. What is this costing you?
5. What are you attached to?
6. What is the dream?
7. What is the essence of the dream?
8. What is beyond this problem?
9. What is ahead?
10. What are you building towards?
11. What has to happen for you to feel successful?
12. What gift are you not being responsible for?
13. What are your healthy sources of energy?
14. What's stopping you?
15. What's in your way?
16. What would make the biggest difference here?
17. What are you going to do?
18. What do you like to do?
19. What can you do to be happy right now?
20. What do you hope to accomplish by having that conversation?
21. What do you hope to accomplish by doing that?
22. What's the first step?
23. What would it be like to have excitement and fear at the same time?
24. What's important about that?
25. What would it take for you to treat yourself like your best client?
26. What benefit/payoff is there in the present situation?
27. What do you expect to have happen?
28. What's the ideal?
29. What's the ideal outcome?
30. What would it look like?
31. What's the truth about this situation?
32. What's the right action?

33. What are you going to do?
34. What's working for you?
35. What would you do differently?
36. What decision would you make from a place of abundance?
37. What other choices do you have?
38. What do you really, really want?
39. What if there were no limits?
40. What aren't you telling me that's keeping me from coaching/helping you?
41. What haven't I asked that I should ask?
42. What needs to be said that has not been said?
43. What are you not saying?
44. What else do you have to say about that?
45. What is left to do to have this be complete?
46. What do you have invested in continuing to do it this way?
47. What is that?
48. What comes first?
49. What consequence are you avoiding?
50. What is the value you received from this meeting/conversation?
51. What is motivating you?
52. What has you hooked?
53. What is missing here?
54. What does that remind you of?
55. What do you suggest?
56. What is underneath that?
57. What part of what I said was useful? And how so?
58. What is this person contributing to the quality of your life?
59. What is it that you are denying yourself right now?
60. What do you need to put in place to accomplish this?
61. What is the simplest solution here?
62. What would help you know I support this/you completely?
63. What happened?
64. What are you avoiding?
65. What is the worst that could happen?

66. What are you committed to?

67. What is your vision for yourself and the people around you?

68. What don't you want?

69. What if you knew?

70. What's your heart telling you? What are you willing to give up?

71. What might you have done differently?

72. What are you not facing?

73. What does this feeling remind you of?

74. What would you do differently if this problem were solved?

75. What does your soul say?

76. What do you need to say goodbye to in order to move forward?

77. What's the payoff for you of not dealing with this issue?

78. Are things as bad as you say they are or are they worse?

79. At what point when you say "yes" are you really feeling "no"?

80. What is the decision you are avoiding?

81. What are you pretending not to know?

82. What are ten things I absolutely need to know about you?

83. What do you want to be able to say about yourself three months from now? One year from now? Three years from now?

84. What is holding you back? What keeps getting in the way?

85. What is one simple thing you could do today to get you closer to your goal? (Right now! Today!)

86. What is your biggest, wildest dream?

87. What keeps you up at night? What do you find yourself continually thinking about when you're in the shower?

88. What has motivated you in the past to reach/achieve difficult goals, make important decisions, or do challenging things? Can we use this as a motivator now?

89. Who can help you with this?

90. What are you tolerating?

91. What has served you in the past? Is it still in effect now?

92. What would you do if you knew you couldn't fail?

93. What part of this goal is yours? What belongs to someone else? What if the goal was all yours?

94. How can I best support you? What do you need most from me?

95. What are you grateful for?

96. What makes your heart sing?

97. What's missing?

98. What do you have to do differently to make this happen?

99. What do you need to put in place to make this happen?

100. When you attain your goal, what will it look like?

101. Who do you know that is already doing this well?

102. What will be the signs that it's time to begin?

103. How will you know that you have succeeded?

104. How will you know when you arrive?

105. What about yourself—do you need to change?

106. What is one thing you need to focus on to get where you want to go?

107. Could you be mistaken? How could you check this out?

108. Does this align with your vision and goals?

109. What is one thing you feel really good about over this past week?

110. What one thing would make the biggest difference right now?

111. What's your belief about this situation?

112. What would you like more of? Less of?

113. What is true about this situation?

114. What are the effects of this on you?

115. What steps would move this forward?

116. How attached are you to the outcome?

117. What is the "should" in this situation?

118. Is this the time to begin?

119. What is the truth about this situation?

120. What is the path of least resistance?

121. Is there another way? Let's brainstorm five to ten other possibilities.

122. What is this costing you?

123. Can you see what is beyond this problem?

124. Can you see what's ahead?

125. Are you open to a completely different way of looking at this?

126. What are your actions saying about this situation?

127. What will happen if you keep doing this for the next ten years?

128. Underneath all of this, what are you really committed to?

129. What is the legacy that you want to leave behind?

130. May I push you on this?

131. So, what's possible here?

132. What opportunities are you not taking advantage of?

133. Who's really in charge here?

134. What are five changes or actions that you can take in the next 30 days that will move you forward?

135. What are you willing to do to make this work?

136. What consumes your time, to the point that it distracts you from attaining your goals?

137. What do you really, really, really, REALLY want?

138. What are you afraid of about this situation?

139. What is the worst that could happen? And if that happened, what's the worst that could happen after that?

140. What is the best that could happen?

141. What are you NOT saying? What are you holding back?

142. Are you pursuing a goal that no longer makes sense?

143. What internal rules and unspoken standards are having a negative impact?

Appendix B
Recommended Reading

Becoming a Conflict Competent Leader, by Craig E. Runde and Tim A. Flanagan

Book Yourself Solid, by Michael Port and Tim Sanders

Full Steam Ahead, by Ken Blanchard and Jesse Stoner

Get Clients Now, by C.J. Hayden

Good to Great, by Jim Collins

Leading With Questions, by Michael Marquardt

Living Your Strengths, by Albert Winesman, Donald Clifton, and Curt Liesveld

Managing Transitions, Making the Most of Change, by William Bridges

Managing Transitions, by William Bridges

May I Have This Dance, by Joyce Rupp

Now, Discover Your Strengths, by Marcus Buckingham and Donald Clifton

QBQ! The Question behind the Question, by John Miller

StrengthsFinder 2.0, by Tom Rath

The 4-Hour Work Week, by Timothy Ferriss

The Art of Possibility, by Rosamund Stone Zander and Benjamin Zander

The Back of the Napkin, by Dan Roam

The Business and Practice of Coaching, by Lynn Grodzki and Wendy Allen

The CoachU Personal and Corporate Training Handbook, by Coach U Inc.

The International Coach Federation, www.coachfederation.org

The Path, by Laurie Beth Jones

The Portable Coach, by Thomas Leonard

The Power of Full Engagement: Managing Energy, Not Time, is the Key to High Performance and Personal Renewal, by Jim Loehr and Ton Schwartz

The Present Future, by Reggie McNeal

Time to Think, by Nancy Kline

References

The International Coach Federation, http://www.coachfederation.org.

Kline, Nancy. *Time to Think*, London: Cassell Illustrated, 1999.

Winesman, Albert L., Donald O. Clifton, and Curt Liesveld. *Living Your Strengths*, New York: Gallup Press, 2003-2004.

Zander, Rosamund Stone and Benjamin Zander. *The Art of Possibility*, London, England: Penguin Books Ltd., 2000.

About the Authors

Dr. J. Val Hastings, MCC, is the Founder and President of Coaching4Today'sLeaders, Coaching4Clergy, Coaching4Groups, and Coaching4BusinessLeaders. Val hired his first coach while he was pastoring at a local United Methodist church. His progress was noticeable by all, and he began to wonder, "What if I adopted a coaching approach to leadership?" In that moment, a vision began to emerge—a global vision of Every Leader a Coach.

Dr. Hastings is the author of numerous books and has developed four coach training programs which are accredited and approved to the highest level by the International Coach Federation. These trainings are offered globally and are offered in many languages, including English, Spanish, Portuguese, and Korean. Graduates of these programs have received all three coaching credentials: ACC, PCC, and MCC.

Val currently holds the designation of Master Certified Coach through the International Coach Federation, its highest coaching designation. He also holds the designation of Professional Mentor-Coach. In addition to teaching at his own programs, Val holds faculty status at Coach University and Faith Evangelical Seminary. In 2006, Val was a presenter at the global gathering of the International Coach Federation and, in 2007, he served as the President of the Philadelphia ICF Chapter.

Trigena H. Halley, PCC, is the founder and owner of Peak Performance CCT, LLC, which she started in 2009 as a way for her to combine her 20+ years of organizational consulting experience with professional coaching. During her professional career, Trigena has held various leadership positions in the global corporate arena, with a focus on talent development, execution of strategy, achievement of financial goals and client satisfaction.

She specializes in leadership coaching, performance improvement, development of leaders, and working with organizations to employ a sustainable culture of performance and results. Her experience spans service, non-profit, manufacturing, corporate, educational and faith-based organizations. Trigena has significant experience training and coaching groups. She has led the development and implementation of large-scale leadership and coach training programs for several global corporate clients. She also offers a wide variety of individual and organizational assessments.

Trigena is a Professional Mentor-Coach and holds the designation of Professional Certified Coach through the International Coach Federation.

Passionate about the great outdoors, Trigena leads experiential leadership programs and women's adventure retreats using the sport of canyoneering. These adventures provide a rich forum for realization of individual potential. She has found nature itself provides the ideal palate for learning and change.

In 1999, Trigena moved to Sandy, Utah, where she spends four seasons a year outdoors—skiing, hiking, running, river rafting and canyoneering slot canyons. She continues to explore the great state of Utah and other exciting destinations with her husband, two children, and friends